TARNISHED TROPHIES

for my athletic family
light, water, food, courage
eternal love

TARNISHED TROPHIES

Debbie Okun Hill

Copyright © Debbie Okun Hill 2014

Library and Archives Canada Cataloguing in Publication

Hill, Debbie Okun, author
   Tarnished trophies / Debbie Okun Hill.

Poems.
ISBN 978-0-88753-528-4 (pbk.)

1. Sports--Poetry. I. Title.

PS8615.I416T37 2013   C811'.6   C2013-907309-4

Editing: Vanessa Shields
Cover image: Skater by Olena Kassian
Design & Layout: Jason Rankin

Published by Black Moss Press at 2450 Byng Road, Windsor, Ontario, N8W 3E8. Canada. Black Moss books are distributed in Canada and the U.S. by Fitzhenry & Whiteside. All orders should be directed there.

Fitzhenry & Whiteside
195 Allstate Parkway
Markham, ON
L3R 4T8

Black Moss would like to acknowledge the generous financial support from both the Canada Council for the Arts and the Ontario Arts Council.

ACKNOWLEDGEMENTS

"A Confession" was first published in an earlier version with the title "Washed Up Poems: A Confession" in *Inscribed, Volume 4, Issue 6* June 2009 and on-line at www.inscribed.org.

"Adjusting His Circadian Rhythm" was first published on the *blue skies poetry* Website www.blueskiespoetry.ca/2009/07/16/adjusting-his-circadian-rhythm/ July 16, 2009 and archived.

"Cycling under an Overcast Sky" received an *Ascent Aspirations* Honourable Mention Award, 2008 and was first published in *Ascent Aspirations Magazine Anthology Five: Spring 2008 Poetry issue*. It was reprinted in *Swaddled in Comet Dust: A Collection of Award-winning Poems*, Beret Days Press, 2008.

"Effervescence" was first published with the title "Effervescence: A Front Crawl Prodigy" in *Tower Poetry*, Summer Edition, Vol. 57 No. 1 Tower Poetry Society Press, 2008.

An earlier version of "Feeling Dehydrated" was first published in *Perspectives Magazine* January 2009.

"Fishing Lines" was first published on www.ambassadorpoetry.yolasite.com/hill3.php The Ambassador Poetry Project Volume 1: Issue 2 December 2009 and reprinted in *EnCompass 1* A Beret Days Book January 2013.

"Going Phishing" received Honourable Mention in 2007 Canadian Poetry Association Annual Poetry Competition and was first published in *Another Trail of Comet Dust: Poems Pulled From Earth*, Beret Days Press, 2011.

An earlier version of "Hockey Sweat" was a judge's selection in the Canadian Author's Association (Niagara Branch) *The Saving Bannister* 27th Annual Anthology Contest 2012. First published in *The Saving Bannister: Niagara Poetry Anthology Volume 27*, Canadian Authors Association (Niagara Branch), 2012.

Earlier versions of "Losing His Appetite for Winning", "Missing His Mate" and "The Last Scrimmage" were first published in *Windsor Review: Special Sports Issue* Vol. 44, No. 1, Spring 2011.

"On the Way to the Cottage" was first published in *POEMATA, Volume 25, Number 01* The Canadian Poetry Association, 2010.

"Speechless Off the Coast of Terschelling" was Runner-up in the Cranberry Tree Press 2006 "As Heard on the 6 o'clock News" themed Poetry Contest and first published in *Reportage*, Cranberry Tree Press, 2006. It was reprinted in *Another Trail of Comet Dust: Poems Pulled From Earth*, Beret Days Press, 2011.

"Train Station" was first published in an earlier version with the title "Stuck at the Train Station" on Bad Poets Club Blog Website Thursday, July 22, 2010.

SPECIAL THANKS

To all the team players: Marty Gervais, publisher of Black Moss Press for believing in my work and pitching the idea for the sports theme; Vanessa Shields, my editor for all her patience and perspiration in polishing my poems; Bunny Iskov, coach and founder of The Ontario Poetry Society for nurturing my love for poetry; the late Peggy Fletcher for being my mentor, inspiration and moral support and all the members of Writers in Transition who cheered me along; Ryan Gibbs, co-host of Sarnia's Spoken Word event and everyone in the audience who were like family to me; the original After Hours Poet Group: Lynn Tait, the late Adele Kearns Thomas, Joe Farina, Rhonda Melanson and Venera Fazio who wrestled the 'little darlings' out of my work and suggested some champion titles; Phyllis Humby and Bob McCarthy for their laughter and friendship; Bryan, Meghan and Mickey for all their love and athletic abilities; my spiritual muse appearing like a ping pong ball out of the clouds; for all the athletes and non-athletes in Ontario and Manitoba and around the world who acted as my template (forgive my creative liberties, all the characters and situations are fictitious) and finally the Ontario Arts Council Writers' Reserve program for providing me with an incentive to work on my next book project *Beneath Ash Canopy: Poems.*

CONTENTS

TRAINING
It Starts Here	10
Thirst for First	12
They are Orange	14
Call in the Zebras	15
Hockey Sweat	17
Hockey Parent Pilgrimage	19
The Last Scrimmage	20
Meltdown of a Sugar Plum Fairy	21
Arrival at Lake Placid, New Year's Day 2009	23
White Picket Fence Dreams	24
English Sports Writer Hibernating in Saint Donat	25
Reaching the Summit	26
Light of Fireflies	28

BUILDING MUSCLE
I Saw Jesus Riding a Bicycle	30
Cycling under an Overcast Sky	32
Spare Tires	34
Road Closed, Detour Ahead	36
On the Way to the Cottage	37
Going Phishing	38
Engaged on the Shoreline	40
Fishing Lines	42
A Confession	44
Effervescence	46
Spilling Warm Lemonade	47

Feeling Dehydrated	49
Trip Diary	50
Train Station	52
Adjusting His Circadian Rhythm	54
Sailing in California	55
Language of the Sea: A Found Poem	56
Speechless Off the Coast of Terschelling	58
Missing His Mate	60
Tackling Laundry	62
Her Last Play In The Soccer Game	64

HITTING HOME

Retaliation After Striking Out	66
Spectator	67
Unrewarded	69
The Gift of Ping Pong	70
Volleying Words	71
Taking a Shot	72
Sharp as Darts	73
Cutting Remarks	74
Boxing Day Punch	75
Wrestling With His Mind	76
Losing His Appetite for Winning	77
Not So Stable	79
At the Click of a Stopwatch	80
The Finish Line	82
A Saline Solution	84
This is Where it Ends	85

TRAINING

IT STARTS HERE

Call it a
horticultural
experiment
an eye dropper
of perspiration
mix of water
sodium, potassium
calcium, magnesium
drizzle-smeared
across athlete's forehead
the front line racers
in this cross country meet
where a god-coach-scientist
plants competitive seeds into
minds of future track stars
young green stolons
seeking nourishment
10-52-10 from wet earth

waiting for starter pistol's
white puff of smoke
quick-click of stopwatch

loud bang like first day of creation

signaling a runner's release
sprinting over soggy leaves
parents nurturing the frenzy
of *"go-go-gold"*
hundreds of voices cheering
in Canatara Park's autumn splendor
a modern day Garden of Eden
with slithering snakes on patrol
ready to trip the weakest warriors

THIRST FOR FIRST

They run with steady pace
long strides like white panthers
in high school uniforms
kinetic movement of limbs
catching the "high-five"
sports fever
chasing each other
along Lake Huron beach,
rolling waves cold stinging
wet sand clinging like
extra hourglass minutes
added to their cleats

Ahead, the paved road
so hard, smooth
black tarred then
wood-chipped trails
up, down, around
Tarzan Lands
beneath
Carolinian canopy
to a finish line

Open-armed field
filled with hugs
pats on the backs
for the top winners
now wearing medals or
bright satin ribbons

The losers wipe
their foreheads
with jersey sleeves
dribble-drip sweat
stains their pride
guzzle-gulped sports drinks
unable to quench
their thirst for first

THEY ARE ORANGE*

Not yellow, not blue, not green
they hoot and holler
can't sit still, stand up,
act first, think later
Who's on first? What's on second?
sporty carriers of the orange flag
this energy boost gushing
rushing through their blood,
an inherited trait, they cannot erase
their personalities, strong, powerful
no couch potato, no lazy label for them
they are fighters and risk takers
competitors, vibrant and hearty
like firm squeeze of a citrus fruit
all driven to the peeled edge
spitting out pith and pip
waving their fists in the air
athletes, loving the succulent
that juicy taste of orange victory

---

* one of four colors representing basic personality temperaments as outlined in the True Colors (personality) Test developed by Don Lowry in 1978

CALL IN THE ZEBRAS

Listen fans to your podcast
there's a zoo out there
on the hockey rink
a bunch of chimps in jersey wear
shaking sticks and making noise
a hungry crowd gone monkey wild
turkey vultures and crazy apes
hooting owls, laughing hyenas
and what's this?
a lone giraffe stomping, yelling
long neck stretching
making things official
two official
three official
four official
it doesn't matter to him
2-1, 1-1, one man
call in the zebras he says
give them a whistle
black helmets, black pants
black skates, white laces
they'll know what to do
these referees,
linesmen and assistants
watching for rule violations
blue lines and red lines

goals and no goals
icings and offside
penalties and more
there's a zoo out there
on the hockey rink
but the zebras are here
let the play begin

HOCKEY SWEAT

Warm water
with a taste of salt,
these bodily fluids
beaded dots on his brow.
No saline solution
to ease the wounds
of his ego-inflamed head.
His high sticking remarks
more like anger at his failure
to perform, to skate his best.
His father screaming *'no way'*
from the top of the stands.
He can hear him scolding,
the tongue lashing he will
receive in the car on the way home.
These repressed droplets
now leaking in slow motion
from his forehead.
The way it dribbles down
like his confidence melting.
This hockey player
who slumps on the
penalty box bench.
His mind turning the other way
refusing to look at his team mates
miffed by his actions on the ice.

So much sweat now
staining his jersey.
The tournament's silver cup
sliding from his fingers.
The cheers of celebration
from the opposing team
as his rival shoots the puck,
scores the winning goal.
One last droplet
splattering on his skate.

HOCKEY PARENT PILGRIMAGE

We are not used to such ice storms
pre-dawn Saturday shivers
wind chills billowing through ski jackets
our ears in toques blocking
winter's whistle cutting through pines

And even when we escape indoors
rub our feet, ten fingers mitten numb
strangers huddling in a barn arena
we are left in frozen pond state
wondering how long this practice
your hockey dreams will last
how your best attempts, a near goal
hockey stick like matchstick
striking net post, your soul still
igniting some dwindling flame desire
your rosy glow immortalized
now searing our hearts
not caring about winning or losing
just wanting to find some warmth
in this Canadian hip checking,
puck pulverizing sport

THE LAST SCRIMMAGE

At first, huddled in mismatched hockey gear
we worship this season of shinny
where there is no outpouring, down pouring
of rain upon nylon umbrellas
no yellow plastic raincoats
no rubber boots to wade in frozen puddles
no quench of thirst to waken the dead
brown blanketed bulbs waiting
in garden graves, black velvet lined tombs
cradling backyard hockey rinks

Winter's frigid stillness hangs like icicles
clear daggers jutting down from eaves
where leaves linger, chilled in ice bath
we scrimmage oblivious to darkening clouds
rumbling bodies skating forward and back
a slap shot, sponge ball, down centre ice
our bruises, a blue line from falling
our knees sore as we get up
reaching for the last sliver of daylight
we rise to score just one more goal
before the outpouring, down pouring
of rain on our slippery slick sticks

MELTDOWN OF A SUGAR PLUM FAIRY

Too many sweets!

She screams with tight fists
trying to kick off her skates
struggling with long laces
like green licorice strings
tied in sticky chain knots
a daunting task for a *prima donna*
five-year old without her mother slave
hovering, doting in crowded change room
her precious "skating world" arena
a Nutcracker fiasco
her round face,
the angry red of a tired plum
her fairy wings
bent from her earlier fall
a failed attempt at a "bunny hop"
a slip, flat on her back
spotlighted, video-taped on ice
a dress rehearsal blunder
her tears no longer suppressed
her outburst, a torrential downpour,
dramatic flood of words and gestures

In contrast, her Godmother caregiver
a lip balm to chapped lips
holds her down, keeps her still
trying to wipe the sugar snow
a powdered layer off sharp bladed tongue
checking the caked icing on her knees
the cracks in her pie-shell
leather skate boots
the crumbs of chocolate dirt
on her pink lacey costume
her *sugar plum* bruised ego,
now wrapped in a Hudson Bay blanket
carried to the car, driven home
where they will cuddle
watch the Olympics together
before drifting asleep

ARRIVAL AT LAKE PLACID, NEW YEAR'S DAY 2009

Darkness swallows
each roadside village
our dim-lit scenic drive
to Lake Placid
sunset fading to black ice sky.

This is where Olympic dreams
were realized and broken
faded memories, 1932, 1980
a place where ghost shadows
inhabit the arenas
the mountain chairlifts,
the snow-banked streets
of our unplanned journey
our downhill skis in tow
Vancouver 2010, still far away
we settle in hotel comfort
wait for morning, bright sun
to raise white blizzard curtain,
to shake the sleet of sleep
to unfold long history of alpine sports
lying dormant in our wintry minds

WHITE PICKET FENCE DREAMS

At one time
suspended in thin air
a moment between
stopwatch seconds
he may have dreamed
of white picket fences
all posts standing straight
like combat soldiers
ready for the Cold War
like Olympic giant slalom hopefuls
braced at the starting gate
on top of Whiteface Mountain
Wilmington, New York

But today ageing pickets tumble
around sunken chest home
yesteryear's groomed athlete
a pendulum no longer swinging
seasonal weather stripping his skin
the rain soaking each fallen point
ice weapons chiseling his bare wood bones
like an army sent onward without any support
like a hockey team defeated
no miracle on ice
returning home to Canada
without carrying a medal

ENGLISH SPORTS WRITER HIBERNATING IN SAINT DONAT

My English words lie dormant
in Saint Donat, Quebec
suffocated by French verbs
hidden beneath crusted snow
stuck in frozen graves
encased in ice blankets
no ink flow of poetic lines
no sports news to report

Yesterday, I took an icicle
"Il fait froid..."
tried to etch a mark
hoping to break through
ice block, locked verse
but blustery wind blew
tripped me, pushed me
with swirling scarf commas
left me lying in blind blizzard
like a hibernating grizzly
curled in a blue period cave
too cold to write anything

REACHING THE SUMMIT

Breathing
so *darn* difficult, slow motion
craving oxygen, another bottle
quick, so much confusion
like sucking air through straws
rocks of ice, an avalanche of cold
pressing, depressing the lungs
damn you, red blood cells, work
weakening, yet p-u-l-l-i-n-g
tugging strength from *Sherpa*,
the ropes, another step
glaciers forming on masked faces
the way the body must adapt
stoic to changing conditions
frigid temperatures and wind gusts
minus 50 degrees Celsius or colder
with strong possibility of white-outs
bundled in thermal parkas
numb hands in thick mitts
heavily socked feet, a must
crampons on boots
one step in front of the other
anchored by long ropes
weighed down by hiking gear
bracing a flag against blustering winds

watching the sun rise like
golden coin over Tibet
no time to celebrate
oxygen limited
visit on summit shortened
the fear of falling, still possible

LIGHT OF FIREFLIES

Darkness descends
and from our balcony window
we watch the lights
dance down the mountain
the flash of giant fireflies
snowmobiles darting
around hydro poles
beacons for everyone

BUILDING MUSCLE

I SAW JESUS RIDING A BICYCLE

Had I stumbled in oven desert sand
HE might have been on camel
traveling towards me from afar
but the coast was too clear
and I was sunning on seaweed
a mermaid out of salt water
and HE the fisherman giant
with rod and tangled line
steered away, towards the shore
rode his bike on the sidewalk
his long chestnut hair
a bouncing mane like
a snagging net along his back

I didn't notice the Jesus boots
those leather sandals they all wore B.C.
still walking on water, performing miracles

Instead he turned away from me
pedaled quick, quicker
as though he remembered
it was I who stuck my gum
between frail pages
of church hymn book
musical notes clinging
hooked so tight
the angels couldn't sing
the organ music cancelled
silenced for another day

CYCLING UNDER AN OVERCAST SKY

On twisting road
towards Menopause
grey clouds linger
like a clogged drain
a broken sieve lined
with newspaper
oppression depression
wet black wheels
of a female cyclist
sliding on pavement
skidding through puddles
the splish-splash droplets
of mud against night sweats
the dampness that soaks
through a t-shirt

So easy to forget
to lose the mind
the agility
to stop pedaling
but nothing pauses
the cycles between
womb somersaults
and the twisting
turning of a sharp shovel
digging lifting heavy clay
thick soil onto a grave

Life changes continues
through chameleon clouds
the revolving
wind-spinning spokes
that cut our hearts
those hidden nails
on a path puncturing
our tired lungs
as we wait for the
silver of sun to
take a seat
grab the handle bars
steer the shine
show the bright reflection
on life's wet chrome

SPARE TIRES

He used to race motocross bikes with his friends,
spend his weekends loading his gear
in the back of an old Ford truck
drive across Ontario to various tracks
returning home with a trophy
and an envelope of cash winnings to place in the bank

His wife used to stay at home, painting images of birds on canvas
watch their backyard deteriorate from her husband's neglect
overgrown lilac bushes, untrimmed *spirea* and climbing roses
the tall grass succumbing to golden rod and Canadian thistle
the patio stones crumbling, house and fence paint peeling
his used tires, a haven for rabbits and field mice

Today, it's diabetes and drastic changes
he sells his motocross bike
she gives away her paint easel and palette
it's supporting each other in new fitness routines

Retired husband pedals his mountain bike
thoughts of his job vanishing
like motocross exhaust of his past

His wife rides a new 10-speed without a helmet
wind's wings twisting her hair, grey locks un-twirling
a sail for her handle bars

Both recycle memories of unwanted spare tires:
jelly rolls of flesh around his and her waistlines
the old motocross tires no longer stacked
like bee-hive honey glazed black donuts
in flimsy cardboard box shed

ROAD CLOSED, DETOUR AHEAD

We are the mechanical camels
chain-linked hoof-print tires
four wheeled speeding
checker-flagged, off-road racing
along uncharted paths
the sand-loving dune-buggies
big-eyed, droopy-eyed headlights
steering left, veering right
out of the seat, bouncing
rumble, rolling hills,
quick sand, oasis
sip-sinking, kneeling drunk
a long drink, flash flooded trails
barricaded, washed out waiting

ON THE WAY TO THE COTTAGE

You see them stranded
aborted trailers
male metal apron strings
cut from a father's fist
the ball and chain
used to drag them
his aluminum baggage of
material status
his sail boat
tall towering
his motorcycle
quick spin of tires
his motor home
barely out of the box

Heavy burden of debt
no match for tiny tires
broken axle succumbed
to extra weight
fallen merchandise
now littering gravel roads

GOING PHISHING

        Outdoors, in outlet absent darkness
we forget about computer sabotage
turn off our *iPods*, flip over a rock
shine our flashlights, battery powered
along black pressed earth
seek out night crawlers
fat worms, squirming bodies
miniature Sumo mud wrestlers
sliding from slippery fingers
        To recharge, we eat breakfast
two thin slices of white bread
a chunk of ham ripped from package
watch pink Dawn open her eyes
our mother, sponge rollers in hair,
yawning, crawling from family tent
scanning, asking what we're doing
so we pause...static in air
Going fishing
and her voice shocks
OOoooo *Wellll...good luck....*
mouth opening like a running carp
That lake's polluted...

      Unplugged once more, we pause
short circuit stare
at gum wrapper filament
silver foil somersaulting
beneath our muddy shoes
we watch the worms
escaping from aluminum cans
we break our twigs
toss our fishing line, tangled
uncoiled copper in rusty tackle box
we kick, SPLASH, turbulent water
dam each current surging
still raging through our minds
the downstreaming of music
caught in our *iPod Shuffles*
as we move on, drifters dreaming
longing for New Wave ways
of phishing on-line

ENGAGED ON THE SHORELINE

So many suitors
sit, stand, stare, whistle,
wait in line to see her
this celebrity bride slow-waltzing
down Lake Huron aisle
a white vision, like a ghost
sailing over blue waters
her wake like white veil
cascading silk, rippling,
trailing behind her
saluting her regal name
Her Majesty's Canadian Ship
Ville de Quebec
her engagement
a mission in Sarnia
early September 2009
raising awareness
for her Canadian Navy
young men and women
dedicated and focused
so many careers,
opportunities available.

Along Point Edward shoreline
a male teen, lone figure
a bachelor, novice fisherman
sits engaged, complacent
meditating, un-groomed
brown hood like monk's robe
pulled over his head
he casts his line
allows his mind to wander
his hook, a rusty edge snagging
unexpected daydreams
his rod and reel pointed
away from zebra mussels
their invasion, not his concern
his hunger pains deepening
the smell of fries, salt and vinegar
swirling scent beneath twin bridges
oblivious to the crowd cheering
Navy's warship bride passing him by.

FISHING LINES

She tangled her words
like matted fishing lines
found along pebbled shore
the strands pale blue as
though the river sucked
the ink out blew the straw color
through the waves
the ones that crested curled
turned frothy white
expired beneath her bare toes

she used to look for answers
in broken sea shells
the skeletal bones
of fish that committed suicide
the ones that choked air
while surfing farther faster
a daring feat landing
stranded on dry land

but even if she could untangle
her mangled thoughts
no words were needed here
not even a whisper tucked
between damp smell of wetness
slimy snails sucking a green path
along moss coated rock
treasure fist of granite pieces
and beer bottle sea glass
the weeds swaying
waving to anyone
silent communication
to those drifting sailors
the ones who survived
swam to the shore to rest

A CONFESSION

I, fisherman poet
not ready to retire
take you, paddle boat,
down Red River
to meet my mistress muse
aquatic gal with seaweed hair
wet one who baits me, lures me
makes me tug hard for words
silver scales of music on her back
underwater dictionary, weak phrases
watered down, washed up
like catfish fighting for air
not wanting to feel sun's glitter
ripping my writer's block
her flesh hook dragging
needing fresh fluid thoughts
rhythm and rhyme
between fins submerged
swimming to further
metaphoric depths where
poetry stirs silt and sand
a sunken ship rises
and I abandon you,
my paddle boat wife,
swap you for

washed up poems
my confession announcing
a deeper love for her

EFFERVESCENCE

From poolside deck chair
at his first swim meet
you twist white plastic cap
like squeezing a lemon
allow wet sour bubbles
to rise like
a soft drink in
light green bottle

And you draw it
closer to your lips
taste crisp spray
splish splash of water
the quench of watching
your son raising his arm
like a victory flag
the one used in
his front crawl
the one crossing
the finish line
of his first
inflatable
wading pool

SPILLING WARM LEMONADE

I remember sinking
soft slow slide
deep in summer's
webbed chair
the way it cushioned
made crisscross imprints
on the back of my thighs
my legs dangling
toes slipping in
cool pool water
your blank stare
distorting your reflection

You were angry that day
spilling your warm lemonade
not saying a word
kicking your thoughts
against wooden fence
hot sun blanketing
blistering your shoulders
the blue faces of
forget-me-nots
shriveled and curled brown

You had forgotten
your favorite sport
the way you swam laps
first your breast stroke
the steady up and down rhythm
your twisted turn, then
a smooth glide off pool wall
your fluttering fin feet
against nature's current

Instead you kept asking
about your lemonade
as your memories spilled
out sticky and thick
like a fog over your empty deck.

FEELING DEHYDRATED

Excuse me, I'm feeling thirsty
clear water within me drained
my insides now empty
my plastic shell rolling
blown over by winds
pecked by free-flying seagulls
nesting in a landfill site

Neighborhood smells reek of
rotting eggs, composting leaves
the stench of banana peels
the rustling of mice
the scrape of metal shovel
near my bottled neck

I am one of many
war camp prisoners
tossed in waste deep heap
awaiting ice chilled daggers
of a hundred raging winters
I am loved and I am hated
caught between two sides
of ongoing controversy
I am thirsty but I will survive
clutter your blue box mind
so you'll never forget to refill
or recycle my million friends

TRIP DIARY

> *The restless rumble of the train,*
> *The drowsy people in the car,*
> *Steel blue twilight in the world,*
> *And in my heart a timid star.*
> —from In the Train
> Sara Teasdale (1915)

We stuff overnight bags with sports gear
athletic socks, sports bras and jockey wear
t-shirts and color-coordinated uniforms
foot powder, razors, lotion, and more
this weekly ritual of gathering and sorting
like black squirrels preparing for winter
scrambling to make arrangements for
car pools, buses and our favorite
The restless rumble of the train,

All together, traveling to out-of-town games
we bounce like basketballs from seat to seat
sharing gossip, truth or dare
humming songs along the way
and when we've had our fill
of chicken breasts and Spanish rice for supper
we collect our sport drink cheers and strategies
lean on each other for mutual support
our tired limbs and sore muscles, joining
The drowsy people in the car,

And before I settle down, brush my hair,
rest my own head on sinking pillows of sleep
in travel diary, I jot silly observations like
The steel blue twilight in the world,

Where dreams of winners and losers converge
and each team respects the other
I pause to catch a glimpse of one last thought
a bright flash, this fastball comet falling quick
an omen landing near my opened window
And in my heart a timid star.

TRAIN STATION

Standing alone, near wooden post
ostracized from adult crowd
young male teen fidgets,
kicks a pebble
outside rural train station
loose gravel crunching
beneath his feet
hot sun searing his cheeks
quick snap-pop, click of teeth
his tongue twirling
juicy piece of bubble gum
grape flavour released
ball cap turned backwards
skateboard shoes untied

In this afternoon game of waiting
he loses valuable playtime
like rolling childhood marbles
on his stepfather's whittle wasting hours
wood-chipped seconds suspended

locomotion   slow

Each yellow dandelion
turning grey between thin cracks
slight breeze unraveling
unnourished seeds of his mind
wandering, blown away

when no one picks him up
leaves him feeling small
reminiscent of his days
hiding as an abused toddler
curled beneath a sports bench
coiled, thick wad, stale
like his gum - stuck
with no place to go

ADJUSTING HIS CIRCADIAN RHYTHM

There is a time, a change in rhythm
almost poetic, a clock ticking
deep within his body, circadian
a movement between dark and light
a time to dream beneath quilt cover
a time to open his eyes
a time to sit on rocks
soak up sun stains on beach lined resort
fill vacation hourglass with sand
slow trickle of crystal granules
slipping through water, riding the tide
full moon reflecting on ocean surface
jet's lag cutting night's sleep
drawing from his exhaustion
lost time in another zone
a white foggy chalk line
against blue surf board sky

SAILING IN CALIFORNIA

Steer my rudder away from the sand
so I can feel the waves
south wind pillowing my blouse
my sail over your horizon

Sprinkle those sparkles of stars
Heaven's sun-drenched light
lifting spirit wisps of hair
leaving my upper mast swaying
fore, main, and mizzen royals
like fronds of a San Diego palm

LANGUAGE OF THE SEA: A FOUND POEM**

Ahoy, seaman to seaman
Morse code and semaphore
our nautical tongue
like mist, a thin wet vapour
a capful of wind
this rendezvous regatta
with racing flags, tall ships
jockeying between guns
all hands on deck
all sails aback
to coil a rope, a yarn
round turn and two half hitches
a gust of wind
Poseidon, god of the sea
navigating Neptune's sheep,
waves breaking into foam
his compass
mounted on gimbals
housed in a binnacle
sailing
round the buoys
hugging the coast
hornpipe, a sailor's dance
running free in blue water

**   Words found in *A Dictionary of Sailing* by F. H. Burgess A Penguin Reference Book, 1961

ease her, stop her, go astern
retire at four bells
a beachcomber, a bird's nest
no safe anchorage
silhouettes of
Schooner, Gunter, and
Bermudian yawl
the eyes of her, docking

SPEECHLESS OFF THE COAST OF TERSCHELLING***

If I could speak from my soul
White tennis court dream
Beach stepped on
Utter, cough, clear my throat
Spit grit sand, raise my voice
Near Oosterend
Terschelling Island, Netherlands
You might hear rumble, roar
Of my thoughts drifting
In broken box along North Sea
Feel my salted wounds from words I bare

If I could whisper my past voyage
I'd share a sea captain's secret
A tale of tipsy terror on ship *Mondriaan*
Wind tossed, trip tipped overboard
My shoelace unwinding
Caught in unexpected storm,
Slip, sip, swallowing water slowly
My thick leather tongue stuck inside,
All thoughts laced up like the others

***   Inspired by a photo/news story about thousands of tennis shoes washed up on the beach near Oosterend on Terschelling Island, Netherlands (The Observer, Saturday, February 11, 2006, page A7)

And we all have similar stories
Unpolished, buried with no voices
A thousand empty shoes, stranded
Like dead soles washed up on shore

MISSING HIS MATE

Last week, he tumble-fell
somersaulted between
two parked vehicles
couldn't feel the ankle
in deserted parking lot
of neighborhood
fitness centre
dark metallic bodies
shade shadowing
his leather exterior
brown autumn decay
leaf caked mud on
tough white skin
all eyes open,
riveted, staring
tongue hanging out
alone, poor sole
his mate out walking
maybe jogging
running around in
nearby football field

And as this season ends
slips between
winter's white sheets
he remains paralyzed,

hurt, empty, cannot get up
hoping someone will find him
put him back where he belongs
nestled inside athletic bag
treasured by all-star trainer
this missing track shoe
flattened yesterday by mini-van
trodden today by careless students

TACKLING LAUNDRY

Last quarter...

   time out

...a coin, silver caribou
inserted in jukebox, clothes
dropped in hotel laundromat
a play by play
where football grime
lingers
      fumble
            tumble
static cling
      spins
with grass-grit stubborn stains.

A loose pair, those jockey socks
dirty souls on white bleached cotton
making a pass, a common move.

Each receiver, a hooker
slightly un-padded but lemon fresh
the sports bra and her clasps
like sharpened fingernails
getting caught on his lint cycle
warning: penalty for a clothesline is 15 yards
dryer setting generating excessive heat
her touch-*Downy* sheets, their end zone.

HER LAST PLAY IN THE SOCCER GAME

At four years young, she sits in middle of soccer field
like dreamy princess floating on cloud turf pillow
attending Alice in Wonderland's tea party, no doubt
picking clumps of dandelions, bright yellow bouquet of weeds
placing them under her nose, sharing them with teammate girlfriend
both wearing forest green jerseys, black shorts,
long game socks and cleats, completely
oblivious to kinetic activity beside them

Their coach, giving up, too busy focusing on future prodigies
those other "I'm having fun" color-coordinated players
running full force like swarm of bees chasing an opponent
then kicking forward and back an inflated soccer ball ego

The princess's parents sigh, first a quiet embarrassment,
then more firmly shaking their heads,
the only ones watching the delinquent pair
trying to chuck-chuckle, make a joke of it,
before thinking about their cheque book,
the expense of extracurricular sports,
the loss of unscheduled playtime
at such a young age

HITTING HOME

RETALIATION AFTER STRIKING OUT

On strike, protesting exercise
in stifling heat, no pickets allowed
just daydreaming on pillow clouds
you roll an imaginary snowball in your mitt
cup the round shape like a baseball
toss it high, then higher
watch it splatter, b-r-e-a-k into ice shards
as it strikes the earth
like a bowling ball
taunting your opponents
knocking all the kingpins down
yelling in their ears
"some strikes are better than others"

SPECTATOR

She stands throwing judgment
without wearing an umpire's mask
lanky arms by her side
her brother's first baseball glove
like a wilting brown cabbage
lying limp in home base dust dirt
her white gym shorts a flag in the breeze
her one shoelace snaking loose near her ankle

They have left her all of them
the spectators no longer cheering
no longer munching hot dogs
no peanuts nor popcorn in the stands
empty coffee cups, plastic water bottles
littering the hardpan, the playing field
tall sparse grass beneath wooden seats

Nine innings ago she was one of them
a speck squeezed in sea of classmates
family friends perhaps scouting agents
all eyes focused on her two older brothers
the hometown pitcher and catcher
one tall lean black hair tucked beneath his cap
the way he spit on the ground with a swiftness
mimicking his trademark fast ball
the other more stout, tendons on legs bulging

67

through socks as he stooped down further and further
catching each throw each girl's kiss from the stand
athletic heroes hailed by sports reporters
uplifted in community papers across the region

Alone she stands staring at the empty diamond
the bases unloaded the smell of steak sizzling
from a nearby barbeque the hum of traffic
cool breeze swirling the dust around her feet

Back home she knew they would be celebrating
opened soda cans pop fizzing on fingers
slaps on her brothers' backs
the way her parents placed
their golden images above her
like trophies lining their upper shelves

At eight years old she could not compete
trying so hard to catch her breath
her asthma aggravated
by late summer ragweed golden rod
no home run, no medals in sight for her
not even a pat on the shoulder
when she entered the spelling bee contest
came home alone with a third place ribbon
something she could treasure with
her stuffed monkey, her *Chatty Cathy* doll
her imaginary cheerleaders
applauding in the silence of her pink laced room

UNREWARDED

Jammed between dirty floor mats
and her evening gymnastics workout
she crushes her raspberries blue
pushes them through metal sieve fence
stirring in starch to thicken
the bubbling somersaulting sauce
the jellies and jams in mason jars
like trophies of gymnasts
golden light weight bodies
collecting dust in basement
memories savored along with
County Fair blue ribbons
her toasting of new beginnings
something sweet on moist lips
preserving her bitten tongue
before she complains too much
and her mind flips lands on her head
exposes her mopped failure
a dismal day
no applause for her housework
no award for her sweeping floor routine

THE GIFT OF PING PONG

Back   and   forth
   back   and   forth
  they argued   for days
back   and   forth
   their words bouncing
 back   and   forth   off
concrete   walls against each other
like two   white   ping   pong balls
they bought with a ping   pong   table
too large to fit in their basement
   ping   pong   ding   dong
the birthday gift for their son
no bicycle bells ringing in his ears
ding   dong   ping   pong
     too large to wrap
and their teen son now shouting
    back and   forth
trying to catch their attention
back and forth   back and forth
    "who cares?"
not worried about the ping pong paddle
even less interested in the ping   pong table
   "I wanted a wii game."

VOLLEYING WORDS

A public school gymnasium
surrounded by sports banners
acknowledging
lingering sweat legacy of
all-star athletes

On the floor, mismatched team
nineteen student writers
exchanging volleyball nets
for long row of tables set
their pencils gliding
volleying words
a bump, a serve, a spike
on rustling paper
steady hum of overhead fans
bright lights like spotlights over
red, yellow, and black gym floor lines
intersecting the creative minds
volleyball stories drawn from research
some rallied from the imagination
the block, the campfire defense
their cheers, voices, actions
all scores recorded in print
like the backs of bubblegum cards
pink inflated facts for others to enjoy

TAKING A SHOT

They take turns shooting dirty looks
a piercing stare through shaded glasses
a gang of gals, like rejected basketball players
lined up in front of an empty hoop target
no fluffy pompoms hiding angry faces
no letters pinned to their sweaters
just tattoos, multiple body piercings
silver earrings hoop-ed on lobes and lips
these cheerless females demanding an audience

Popular by scare tactics, they
try to impress their Facebook fans
listing number of athletes they've slept with
settling some teenage drama score by
defacing their victims with bruises
going home under-aged celebrating
with another shot of tequila
thinking they are heroes in a flip cup game
not sore hangover losers
slam dunked later in toilet bowl
victims of some other drunk tank party

SHARP AS DARTS

He screams obscenities
pressing his target
a black and yellow dart board
against outer wall
his vocal darts like competitive jabs
those bullshit remarks still clinging
stuck onto pock-marked cork
his real opponent
the guy who won the dart tournament
manages to escape without a bruised eye
running off with the coveted prizes
thick wad of swindled cash and his girlfriend
(the blonde with the leather skirt)
who conspired it all

CUTTING REMARKS

We have only heard of places
like Afghanistan, India
Pakistan, Korea, and Guyana
the way they fight
sometimes with knives or guns
sometimes with bold flat kites
crushed glass on hemp strings
eager to cut the opponent's line
the tension to control,
a release, a pull, a capture
words spoken and unspoken
a kite runner like a scavenger
seeking what's left

Our fights are not like that
there are no public displays
no blood shed, no cutting remarks
we crawl away into dark rooms
curl like caterpillar commas
our silence spinning a woolen bed
we hibernate, wait for spring
when ice cubed differences unthaw
spilling rainwater
aqua therapy indoors

BOXING DAY PUNCH

She looks away
sunken treasure chest
blue eyes bruised
a colored bulb,
broken filament of light
burnt edges of chicken skin
smear of gravy on
cracked punch bowl

He rumples a newspaper
jaded sports section
crushed angel wing
corner of wrapping
igniting anger
his match burning
beyond raging fireplace
setting aflame
the empty boxes
their remains of Christmas
and his boxing career

WRESTLING WITH HIS MIND

A wrestling match, three rounds
with holds and throws
a pin, shoulders to the mat
a tangled mess of arms and legs
this out-of-body experience
wrestling with his personality
the id, the ego, the superego
thinking, dueling
Which one of you
invented the argument?
red boxing gloves wrapped
around your fists?
Bobo the Roly Poly Clown
a punching bag
hot air covered in plastic?

Who started the fight?
Pulled out sharpened switchblade
the brass knuckles and
cutting remark machetes?
Was it you, my friend
another high school wrestler?
young university fencer?
the skeet shooter?
the non-athletic kid
with buzz cut hair
trying to fit in?

LOSING HIS APPETITE FOR WINNING

He took a chance with steroids
former high school track star boasting
a heart stopping, muscle-building
power trip to instant fame
always tip toe running from drug testing
his medicated habit
a variation of Russian roulette
his only other form of entertainment
watching blockbuster movies
alone during daylight hours
his brown *hoodie*
pulled over his head
his pretzel-shaped body
slumped in theatre seat
of downtown darkened dive.

This famous player's rendezvous
imitating Hollywood's best
the lead, some dashing *007* agent
his own bloodshot eye terror
focusing on silver bullet screen
both bargaining for their lives
not thinking of the consequences
the ambush of machine gun fire
like his own life mirrored
a secret mission smashed

as he staggers out of the theater
still trembling, unsteady on his feet
his appetite for winning lost
vowing to eschew his drug habit
his addiction, his sudden paranoia
the gastric irritation flaring
not knowing whether he can still
leap frog over life's fenced hurdles
that sun block
his blurry finish line

NOT SO STABLE

Sometimes when she stirs, he pauses
    (forgets what he is doing)
her unsaddled back un-brushed
his spurs of impatience upsetting her
how the evening sky darkens
a soft blue bleeding into mystic orange,
flaring red into starlit black cloak.

She knows her Master isn't well
the way his knees rattle
how he buckles with pain
canceling evening rides
(no more wild white daisies
no romp in Queen Anne's lace
just quiet staring at uneaten food)
his jockey sweat, a salt taste mingling
with sweet smell of hay
still yearning, breathing
his heart frail like thin filament
a single light bulb flickering,
the shadow of her stirrup
a haunting noose image
swaying from barn rafters.

AT THE CLICK OF A STOPWATCH

He turned a corner, hanged himself
just like that, click of a stopwatch

another athlete gone

   no graphic details shared
   just rumours haunting
   racing through darkened halls
   a high school student
   well-liked, brilliant star
   a former science fair winner
   an athlete housing so many skills
   well-rounded, balanced
   like the lacrosse ball
   he 'crosse' pocket caught
   during practices and games

this sudden loss of life
unexplained to the masses
all his friends and wannabe pals
expressing their deep sorrow, condolences
and *may he rest in peace* slogans
the Facebook petitions signed by so many
a lengthy article in the local newspaper
stressing the need for more education
the need for more suicide awareness
and parents everywhere, trying to understand
how to keep the human race, the stopwatch ticking
to strike a balance between school and work
sports and leisure activities in
this confused and changing world.

THE FINISH LINE

*So those who are last will be first,
and those who are first will be last.*
   — *Matthew 20:16*

In this obstacle race, steeplechase with horses
she cannot run from the black stallion
his flaring nostrils, a clutch of death
upheld by his team of immortal jockeys
they are buried in the ash
at the base of the church steeple
his hoof prints, their haunting voices
rising like waves, surfing behind her
chasing her like vicious sundogs
nipping at her ankles

Turn this way, turn that way
she tries to escape, to lose them
to hide in her whirling cloud dust

Each hour, she runs through her daily life
attempting to create a better world
where Olympic torches lead athletes
away from gutters and ditches
dark bowling over lanes
unsafe alleyways

Confused, she pauses, catches her breath
as if the phoenix feather
the wings of Pegasus she carries
can survive, can stay preserved
in the cup of her hands
these rewards of winning
in becoming first, in pushing forward
over the rapids, across the deep valley
how quick will they lead her
to death's finish line?

She hears the hoof prints, she teeters on the edge
this is a race, a line she refuses to cross

A SALINE SOLUTION

Like ointment, *aloe vera*
you sprinkle salt, white crystals
into an enamel bowl of tepid water
coax me to dip my athletic foot
torn flesh ripped by nail
into warm solution
a silky soft flow of liquid
washing red blood memories
sealing, healing the wound
the image of Japanese windsocks
wrapped loosely, flying high
navigating south winds

Good luck and longevity
now walking above clouds

THIS IS WHERE IT ENDS

It ends here... *perhaps not*
on the "x", the treasure-seeking spot
where your athletic spirit is standing
somewhere near a garage sale table or
lower shelf of Value Village
undusted unappreciated trophies of
tarnished men and women
molded in various fitness poses
name plates with awards
and winners scratched out
as if they never existed

If you're still half-buried,
recently cremated
still smoking hot,
rolling in your grave
bowling *lucky strikes*
someone may save your
memory from the gutter
resurrect your shiny pin image
keep you polished
like all-star immortal heroes
pulled down from night skies
preserved in oversized mason ware
large glass cases displayed

in high school and arena walls
or type-faced in history books
with all your vital statistics

For those still living inside a dream
collecting banners, photos,
hockey cards and other
sports memorabilia
or those who leave Earth's arena
believing in
the persistence of memory
it may never end
like a Salvador Dali painting
stretching your imagination
the stopped watch keeps ticking
despite the melting of second hands
the hours, their arms still bending,
wrestling in another
time warped existence

listen…a steady drumming
of souls and cleats
against hourglass sand

somewhere lost in the heavens
the race continues

THIS IS WHERE IT ENDS

It ends here... *perhaps not*
on the "x", the treasure-seeking spot
where your athletic spirit is standing
somewhere near a garage sale table or
lower shelf of Value Village
undusted unappreciated trophies of
tarnished men and women
molded in various fitness poses
name plates with awards
and winners scratched out
as if they never existed

If you're still half-buried,
recently cremated
still smoking hot,
rolling in your grave
bowling *lucky strikes*
someone may save your
memory from the gutter
resurrect your shiny pin image
keep you polished
like all-star immortal heroes
pulled down from night skies
preserved in oversized mason ware
large glass cases displayed

in high school and arena walls
or type-faced in history books
with all your vital statistics

For those still living inside a dream
collecting banners, photos,
hockey cards and other
sports memorabilia
or those who leave Earth's arena
believing in
the persistence of memory
it may never end
like a Salvador Dali painting
stretching your imagination
the stopped watch keeps ticking
despite the melting of second hands
the hours, their arms still bending,
wrestling in another
time warped existence

listen...a steady drumming
of souls and cleats
against hourglass sand

somewhere lost in the heavens
the race continues

Debbie Okun Hill is Past President of The Ontario Poetry Society, an Associate Member of The League of Canadian Poets, and for eight years has been a co-host of a monthly open mic event in southwestern Ontario. From her first assignments in rural Manitoba as editor of her high school newspaper/yearbook to her work as a journalist for several rural newspapers and later as a communications specialist with The Winnipeg Art Gallery, Lakehead University in Thunder Bay and Fanshawe College in London, Debbie has accumulated many publishing credits. Since turning to poetry in 2003, over 270 of her poems have been published in over 105 different publications/websites including *Descant, Existere, Vallum, The Windsor Review,* and *Other Voices* in Canada plus *Mobius, The Binnacle* and *Still Point Arts Quarterly* in the United States. She has read her work throughout Ontario including the Fringe Stage of the 2011 Eden Mills Writers' Festival and during the 2012 PoeTrain Express/Spring Pulse Poetry Festival in Cobalt. This is her first full collection of poems by a trade publisher.

PUBLISHED CHAPBOOKS:

Swaddled in Comet Dust: A Collection of Award-winning Poems, The Stanza Break Chapbook Series #27, Beret Days Press, 2008, ISBN 978-1-897497-10-4 24-pages
Another Trail of Comet Dust: Poems Pulled from Earth, The Stanza Break Chapbook Series #43, Beret Days Press, 2011, ISBN 978-1-897497-53-1 24-pages

PUBLISHED ANTHOLOGIES:

EnCompass I, a 75-page anthology featuring the work of Canadian poets Josie Di Sciascio-Andrews, Debbie Okun Hill, Bernice Lever, Lynn Tait and Jan Wood; Beret Days Press, 2013, ISBN 978-1-897497-73-9

The Black Moss Press First Lines Poetry series is for writers who are publishing their first book of poetry.

Books in the First Lines series include:

#1   Now That We Know Who We Are
         by Carlinda D'Alimonte

#2   Moon Sea Crossing
         by Lynn Harrison

#3   What Somone Wanted
         by Shirley Graham

#4   Swimming in the Dark
         by Ross Belot

#5   holy cards: dead women talking
         by Penny Anne Beaudoin

#6   Do Not Call Me by My Name
         by Lisa Shatzky

#7   in lieu of flowers
         by Peter Hrastovec

#8   Glass Beads
         by Sandra Lynn Lynxleg

#9   I am That Woman
         by Vanessa Shields

#10   Tarnished Trophies
         by Debbie Okun Hill

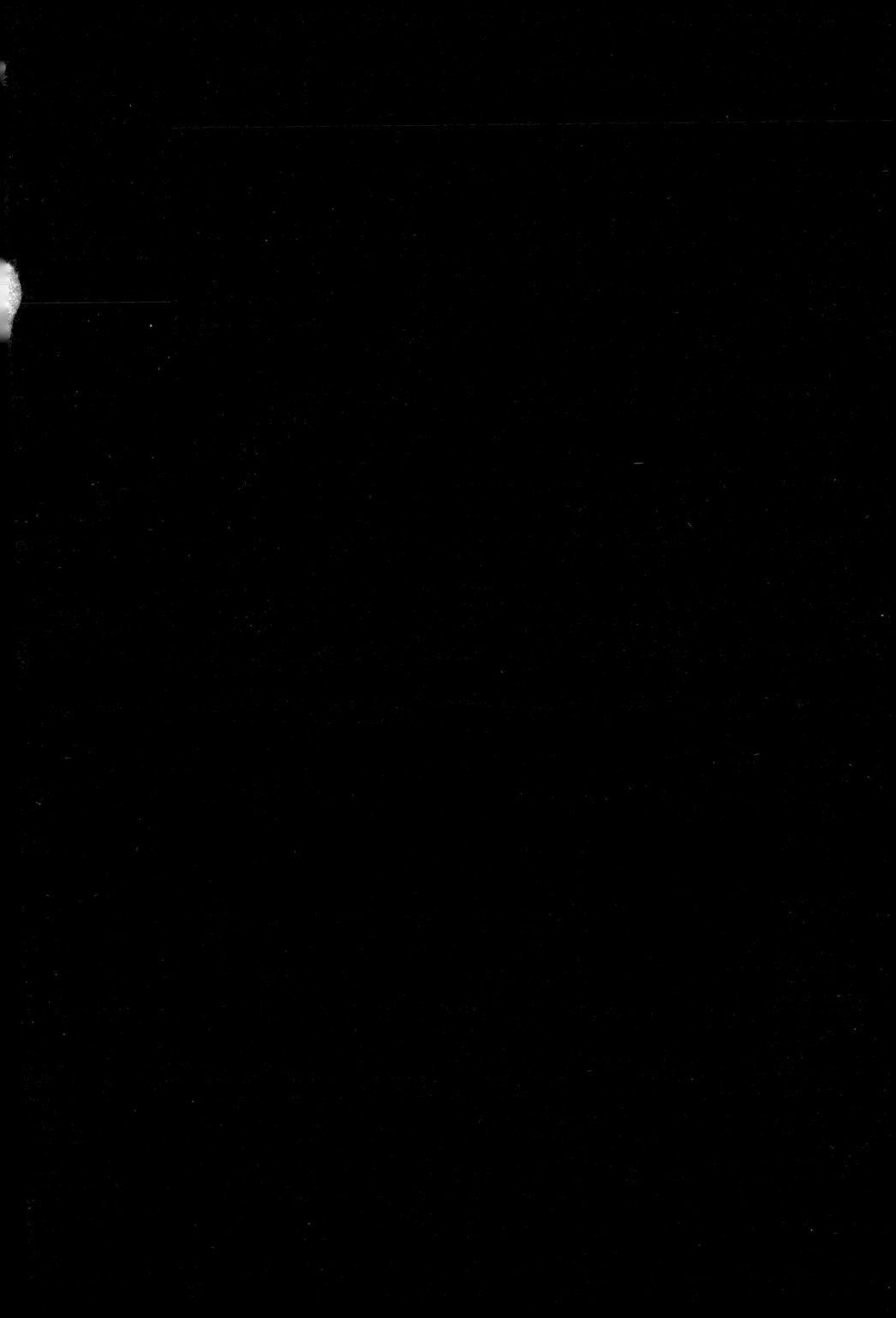